DATE DUE

AO 5 00			

DEMCO 38-296

And Then She Said ....

Quotations by Women for Every Occasion

Compiled by J.D. Zahniser

Caillech Press

© 1989 by J.D. Zahniser.

Originally published by Caillech Press, 1989.
Second edition September, 1990.

Published in the United States by Caillech Press,
482 Michigan Street, St. Paul, MN 55102.

Cover design and illustration by Chris Holzer
Text typefaces: Helvetica and Kaufmann Bold.
Laser typesetting by Business Express, Minneapolis.
Printed by Pocono Press, Cresco, PA.

ISBN 0-9624836-1-3

Table of Contents

Preface

During the last twenty years, women have re-awakened to the need to listen to one another. We have found new sources of inspiration in the words of the woman next door and woman halfway across the world. We have discovered the diversity of women's lives and experiences in the profusion of writing which has marked the emergence of the women's movement.

Since my teenage years, I have copied quotations which moved me from books and magazines, posters and other sources. I have used sayings to spark my own soul and those of students, colleagues, and program participants.

Recently, I realized that no feminist multicultural resource existed for those of us looking for quotes to use in our personal and work lives. Even books of sayings focused on women tend to be sexist, using overwhelmingly white and many male sources.

<u>And Then She Said</u> is designed for people seeking a world of diversity and equality. Its language is gender-sensitive(no generic <u>he</u>'s) and culture-sensitive. You will find authors and activists, celebrities and everyday people in these pages. The multicultural component is significant but not impressive; I hope successive editions of this work will be even stronger in this regard. I hope many of the quotations will touch you as they have me.

And Then She Said is the first publication of **Caillech Press**. The Caillech(or Cailleach) is familiar in Celtic legend as a wise woman and daughter of the moon. The Caillech was known for her ability to shift shape and move mountains.

Caillech Press will continue to produce publications to meet the practical needs of people working to improve women's lives and status.

My thanks to JoAnn Holland and Dick Morrison for assistance in the planning stages of **And Then She Said**.

Jill Diane Zahniser, Ph.D.
October 1989

And Then She Said....
Quotations by Women
for Every Occasion

Aging

We turn not older with years, but newer
every day.

Emily Dickinson, Letters

One keeps forgetting old age up to the very
brink of the grave.

Colette, My Mother's House

We older women who know we aren't heroines
can offer our younger sisters, at the very least,
an honest report of what we have learned and
how we have grown.

Elizabeth Janeway in Ms. 1973

Being middle-aged is a nice change from being
young.

Dorothy Canfield Fisher

In very truth the days are almost free, and if
it is another way of saying that our lives are
empty, well--there are days when emptiness is
spacious, and non-existence elevating . . .

Florida Scott-Maxwell
The Measure of My Days

Every time I think that I'm getting old, and
gradually going to the grave, something else
happens.

Lillian Carter, Ms. 1976

In youth we learn; in age we understand.

Marie Ebner-Eschenbach

It must become a right of every person to die of old age. And if we secure this right for ourselves we can, coincidentally, assure it for the planet.

Alice Walker, <u>Living by the Word</u>

The older one grows, the more one likes indecency.

Virginia Woolf, <u>Monday or Tuesday</u>

Time and trouble will tame an advanced young woman, but an advanced old woman is uncontrollable by any earthly force.

Dorothy L. Sayers, <u>Clouds of Witness</u>

Time is a dressmaker specializing in alterations.

Faith Baldwin
<u>Face Toward the Spring</u>

America

In order to be able to live at all in America I must be unafraid to live anywhere in it, and I must be able to live in the fashion and with whom I choose.

Alice Walker
<u>In Search of Our Mother's Gardens</u>

U.S. politics is a beautiful fraud that has been imposed on the people for years, whose practitioners exchange gelded promises for the most valuable thing their victims own, their votes.

Shirley Chisholm, Unbought and Unbossed

Over increasingly large areas of the United States, spring now comes unheralded by the return of the buds, and the early mornings are strangely silent where once they were filled with the beauty of bird song.

Rachel Carson, Silent Spring

We grew up founding our dreams on the infinite promise of American advertising. I still believe that one can learn to play the piano by mail and that mud will give you a perfect complexion.

Zelda Fitzgerald, Save Me The Waltz

I'm not interested in pursuing a society that uses analysis, research, and experimentation to concretize their vision of cruel destinies for those who are not bastards of the Pilgrims; a society with arrogance rising, moon in oppression, and sun in destruction.

Barbara Cameron
This Bridge Called My Back

Aspirations

I do not want to die until I have faithfully made the most of my talent and cultivated the seed that was placed in me until the last small twig has grown.

Kathe Kollwitz, <u>Diaries and Letters</u>

I might have been born in a hovel, but I determined to travel with the wind and stars.

Jacqueline Cochran, <u>The Stars at Noon</u>

Mama exhorted her children at every opportunity to "jump at de sun." We might not land on the sun, but at least we would get off the ground.

Zora Neale Hurston, <u>Dust Tracks on a Road</u>

I never notice what has been done. I only see what remains to be done.

Marie Curie

We must find our duties in what comes to us, not in what might have been.

George Eliot

Belief & Faith

All outward forms of religion are almost use-
less, and are the causes of endless strife . . .
Believe there is a great power silently working
all things for good, behave yourself and never
mind the rest.   Beatrix Potter, Journal

Hope says to us constantly, "Go on, go on,"
and leads us to the grave.
                              Françoise de Maintenon

The best religion is the most tolerant.
                              Delphine de Girardin

If God is male, then male is God. The divine
patriarch castrates women as long as he is
allowed to live on in the human imagination.
                      Mary Daly, Beyond God the Father

Children / Family

What its children become, that will the community become.   Suzanne LaFollette, Concerning Women

Everywhere, everywhere, children are the
scorned people of the earth.   Toni Morrison
            quoted in Conversations with American Writers

If responsibility for the upbringing of children is to continue to be vested in the family, then the rights of children will be secured only when parents are able to make a living for their families with so little difficulty that they may give their best thought and energy to the child's development and the problem of helping it adjust itself to the complexities of the modern environment.

Suzanne LaFollette, <u>Concerning Women</u>

Our children are not treated with sufficient respect as human beings, and yet from the moment they are born they have this right to respect. We keep them children far too long, their world separate from the real world of life.

Pearl S. Buck, <u>My Several Worlds</u>

One of the things I've discovered in general about raising kids is that they really don't give a damn if you walked five miles to school. They want to deal with what's happening now.

Patty Duke, <u>Call Me Anna</u>

Absence is one of the most useful ingredients of family life, and to dose it rightly is an art like any other.

Freya Stark

Criticism / Praise

A woman of honor should not suspect another of things she would not do herself.

Marguerite de Valois

I praise loudly; I blame softly.

Catherine II

We are valued either too highly or not high enough; we are never taken at our real worth.

Marie Ebner-Eschenbach

Equality

The most mediocre of males feels himself a demigod as compared with women.

Simone de Beauvoir, The Second Sex

There's no question in my mind but that rights are never won unless people are willing to fight for them.

Eleanor Smeal
1985 speech to National Press Club

Men, their rights and nothing more; women their rights and nothing less.

Susan B. Anthony
Used as motto of The Revolution journal

No one can make you feel inferior without your consent.

Eleanor Roosevelt

Class supremacy, male supremacy, white supremacy--it's all the same game. If you're on top of someone, the society tells you you are better.

Coletta Reid and Charlotte Bunch
Class and Feminism

Let women be provided with living strength of their own. Let them have the means to attack the world and wrest from it their own subsistence, and their dependence will be abolished--that of man also.

Simone de Beauvoir, The Second Sex

Many women do not recognize themselves as discriminated against; no better proof could be found of the totality of their conditioning.

Kate Millett, Sexual Politics

On the road to equality there is no better place for blacks to detour around American values than in foregoing its example in the treatment of its women and the organization of its family life.

Eleanor Holmes Norton
quoted in Sisterhood is Powerful

We cannot expect in the immediate future that all women who seek it will achieve full equality of opportunity. But if women are to start moving towards that goal, we must believe ourselves or no one else will believe in us; we must match our aspirations with the competence, courage and determination to succeed.

Rosalyn Yalow
quoted in The Decade of Women

The dogma of woman's complete historical subjection to men must be rated as one of the most fantastic myths ever created by the human mind.

Mary Ritter Beard
Woman as a Force in History

Theories and goals of education don't matter a whit if you don't consider your students to be human beings.

Lou Ann Walker
A Loss for Words: The Story of Deafness in a Family

Whatever women must do they must do twice as well as men to be thought half as good. Luckily, this is not difficult.

attributed to Charlotte Whitton
Mayor of Ottawa

Women are the cowards they are because they have been semi-slaves for so long.

Doris Lessing, A Small Personal Voice

Whether women are better than men I cannot say--but I can say they are certainly no worse.

Golda Meir

Women want mediocre men, and men are working hard to be as mediocre as possible.

Margaret Mead

Freedom

Until economic freedom is attained for everybody, there can be no real freedom for anybody.

Suzanne LaFollette, Concerning Women

Freedom is fragile and must be protected. To sacrifice it, even as a temporary measure, is to betray it.

Germaine Greer, The Female Eunuch

But standing alone we learned our power; we repudiated man's counsels forevermore and solemnly vowed that there should never be another season of silence until we had the same rights everywhere on this green earth, as man.

Elizabeth Cady Stanton
The History of Woman Suffrage

The liberation of women is above all based on their capacity to think their own problems through and to link them to the total progress of the society and the world in which they live, to their capacity to develop a political and cultural consciousness.

Nawal El Saadawi, Sisterhood is Global

Who ever walked behind anyone to freedom? If we can't go hand in hand, I don't want to go.

Hazel Scott quoted in Ms.

Future

But now all I need in order to have a future, is to design a future I can manage to get inside of.

Francine Julian Clark
"Eligible Impulses" in A Wider Giving

Each arc of colour may be lovely to behold, but it is the full spectrum of our woman rainbow that glows with the brightest promise of better things to come.

Merlin Stone, Ancient Mirrors of Womanhood

It has been proved that the land can exist without the country--and be better for it; it has not been proved that the country can exist without the land.

Alice Walker, Living by the Word

The future belongs to those who believe in the beauty of their dreams.

Eleanor Roosevelt

The future is made of the same stuff as the present.

Simone Weil
On Science, Necessity, and the Love of God

Things which matter cost money, and we've got to spend the money if we do not want to have generations of parasites rather than generations of citizens.

Barbara Jordan
I Dream A World

Thus far, women have been the mere echoes of men. Our laws and constitutions, our creeds and codes, and the customs of social life are all of masculine origin. The true woman is as yet a dream of the future.

Elizabeth Cady Stanton
quoted in The History of Woman Suffrage

Gender Roles/Relations

As far as I'm concerned, being any gender is a drag.

Patti Smith
quoted in The Men Say/The Women Say

Lesbian is the word, the label, the condition that holds women in line. When a woman hears this word tossed her way, she knows she is stepping out of line.

Radicalesbians
"The Woman-Identified Woman"

Young boys plan for what they will achieve and attain, young girls plan for whom they will achieve and attain . . .

Charlotte Perkins Gilman
Women and Economics

The keeping of an idle woman is a badge of superior social status. Man must work, and woman must exploit his labor . . . And if the woman submits, she can be cursed for exploitation; and if she rebels, she can be cursed for compeling with the male; whatever she does will be wrong.

Dorothy L. Sayers

People are just not very ambitious for women still. Your son you want to be the best you can. Your daughters you want to be happy.

Alexa Canady, I Dream A World

It began, they say, with Sappho and her dreaming students in the long-ago vales of Lesbos . . . I know it did not stop there . . . all women sense its light lyric touch. For myself, I know only it is part and parcel in my tangled tired coil.

Mary MacLane, The Story of Mary MacLane

A woman's sense of time must be quite different from a man's. Her sense of continuity is internal and natural . . . She connects directly to the source of time, and the moon that pulls the tides around the world also pulls the hormone tide within her; her months are marked off without need of calendar. She carries her months, her years, her spring and winter within her.

Abigail Lewis
quoted in <u>A Day at a Time</u>

A true conception of the relation of the sexes will not admit of conqueror and conquered; it knows of but one great thing; to give of one's self boundlessly, in order to find one's self richer, deeper, better.

Emma Goldman

Just as the difference in height between males is no longer a realistic issue, now that lawsuits have been substituted for hand-to-hand encounters, so is the difference in strength between men and women no longer worth elaboration in cultural institutions.

Margaret Mead
<u>Sex and Temperament</u>

Men fear women's strength.

Anais Nin, <u>Diary</u> volume 3

A man has to be called Joe McCarthy to be called ruthless. All a woman has to do is put you on hold.

Marlo Thomas quoted in <u>Ms</u>.

Boys and girls are expected to behave differently to each other, and to people in general,--a behavior to be briefly described in two words. To the boy we say, "Do"; to the girl, "Don't."

Charlotte Perkins Gilman
<u>Women and Economics</u>

Right now the sweet white bush clover is blooming, but sooner or later winter will come, and the flowers and the stems will dry up. Just wait and see. The relationship between men and women is like this, I guess.

Hayashi Fumiko
quoted in <u>To Live and To Write</u>

The grim possibility is that she who "hides her brains" will, more than likely, end up with a mate who is only equal to a woman with "hidden brains" or none at all.

Lorraine Hansberry
"In Defense of the Equality of Men"
in <u>The Norton Anthology of Literature By Women</u>

For him she is sex--absolute sex, no less. She is defined and differentiated in reference to men and not he in reference to her; she is the incidental, the inessential as opposed to the essential. He is the Subject, he is the Absolute--She is the Other.

Simone de Beauvoir, <u>The Second Sex</u>

Historically our own culture has relied for the creation of rich and contrasting values upon many artificial distinctions, the most striking of which is sex . . . if we are to achieve a richer culture, rich in contrasting values, we must recognize the whole gamut of human potentialities, and so weave a less arbitrary social fabric, one in which each diverse human gift will find a fitting place.

Margaret Mead
<u>Sex and Temperament</u>

A desire to have all the fun is nine-tenths of the law of chivalry.

Dorothy L. Sayers, <u>Gaudy Night</u>

In our steady insistence on proclaiming sex-distinction we have grown to consider most human attributes as masculine attributes, for the simple reason that they were allowed for men and forbidden to women.

Charlotte Perkins Gilman
<u>Women and Economics</u>

Happiness & Sorrow

It is better to learn early of the inevitable depths, for then sorrow and death take their proper place in life, and one is not afraid.

Pearl S. Buck, <u>My Several Worlds</u>

The thinkers of the world should by rights be guardians of the world's mirth.

Agnes Repplier

Keep your face to the sunshine and you cannot see the shadow.

Helen Keller

What happiness is there which is not purchased with more or less of pain?

Margaret Oliphant

Too much of a good thing can be wonderful.

Mae West

Those who do not know how to weep with their whole heart don't know how to laugh either.

Golda Meir

Health/Safety/Procreation

Disease is an experience of so-called mortal mind. It is fear made manifest on the body.

Mary Baker Eddy, Science and Health

If men could become pregnant, abortion would be a sacrament.

attributed to Florynce Kennedy

Laughter is by definition healthy.

Doris Lessing
The Summer Before the Dark

There must be quite a few things a hot bath won't cure, but I don't know many of them.

Sylvia Plath, The Bell Jar

My purpose in this book has been to give rape its history. Now we must deny it a future.

Susan Brownmiller, Against Our Will

Pornography is the instruction; rape is the practice, battered women are the practice, battered children are the practice.

Gloria Steinem
quoted in The Women Say/The Men Say

The door behind which the battered wife is trapped is the door to the family home.

Del Martin, <u>Battered Wives</u>

To label family planning and legal abortion programs "genocide" is male rhetoric, for male ears.

Shirley Chisholm, <u>Unbought and Unbossed</u>

Health is not a condition of matter, but of Mind.

Mary Baker Eddy
<u>Science and Health</u>

No woman can call herself free who does not own and control her body. No woman can call herself free until she can choose consciously whether she will or will not be a mother.

Margaret Sanger

Though woman needs the protection of one man against his whole sex, in pioneer life, in threading her way through a lonely forest, on the highway, or in the streets of the metropolis on a dark night, she sometimes needs, too, the protection of all men against this one.

Elizabeth Cady Stanton
<u>History of Woman Suffrage</u>

We know that every woman wants to be thin. Our images of womanhood are almost synonymous with thinness.

Susie Orbach
quoted in <u>The Obsession</u>

I believe that every woman's soul is haunted by the spirits of earlier women who took risks and resisted as women today are fighting their rapists and batterers.

Adrienne Rich
quoted in <u>The Women Say/The Men Say</u>

History

Like their personal lives, women's history is fragmented, interrupted; a shadow history of human beings whose existence has been shaped by the efforts and the demands of others.

Elizabeth Janeway
<u>Women: Their Changing Roles</u>

So long has the myth of feminine inferiority prevailed that women themselves find it hard to believe that their own sex was once and for a very long time the superior and dominant sex. In order to restore women to their ancient dignity and pride, they must be taught their own history, as the American blacks are being taught theirs.

Elizabeth Gould Davis
<u>The First Sex</u>

Invention of Self

She had nothing to fall back on; not maleness, not whiteness, not ladyhood, not anything. And out of the profound desolation of her reality she may well have invented herself.

Toni Morrison

I am playing with my Self, I am playing with the world's soul, I am the dialogue between my Self and <u>el espiritu del mundo.</u> I change myself, I change the world.

Gloria Anzaldua
<u>Borderlands/LaFrontera: The New Mestiza</u>

You need only claim the events of your life to make yourself yours. When you truly possess all you have been and done, which may take some time, you are fierce with reality.

Florida Scott-Maxwell, <u>The Measure of My Days</u>

Involvement in Life

Considering how dangerous everything is nothing is really very frightening.

Gertrude Stein
<u>Everybody's Autobiography</u>

Walk the street with us into history. Get off the sidewalk.

Dolores Huerta

I see life sometimes as a bird flying. I see a
soul on the wing through a trackless storm,
and every now and again there is a lull and
the bird comes to rest on land. These contacts
with the earth before departing into the storm
again I see as the moments in life when I knew
the meaning. And even though between them I
have my share of storm with everyone else, I
am comforted always by the knowledge that
there is land below, because I have seen it. I
am inspired to go on because I have seen the
meaning myself.

Sylvia Ashton-Warner, <u>Teacher</u>

When you make a world tolerable for yourself, you make a world tolerable for others.

Anais Nin, <u>Diary</u> volume 5

The biggest sin is sitting on your ass.

Florynce Kennedy
quoted in <u>Ms.</u> 1973

One sees that dead, vacant look steal sometimes over the rarest, finest of women's faces,
--in the very midst, it may be, of their warmest
summer's day; and then one can guess at the
secret of intolerable solitude that lies hid be-
neath the delicate laces and the brilliant smile.

Rebecca Harding Davis
<u>Life in the Iron Mills</u>

The true way to soften one's troubles is to solace those of others.

Françoise de Maintenon

One had better die fighting against injustice than die like a dog or a rat in a trap.

Ida B. Wells, Crusade for Justice

Knowledge

Believe only half of what you see and nothing that you hear.

Dinah Mulock Craik

If we had a keen vision and feelings of all ordinary human life, it would be like hearing the grass grow and the squirrel's heartbeat, and we should die of that roar which lies on the other side of silence.

George Eliot quoted in Women's Ways of Knowing

I had never been as resigned to ready-made ideas as I was to ready-made clothes, perhaps because although I couldn't sew, I could think.

Jane Rule
Lesbian Images

It takes a lot of time to be a genius--you have to sit around so much doing nothing, really doing nothing.

Gertrude Stein
Everybody's Autobiography

The ability to think straight, some knowledge of the past, some vision of the future, some skill to do useful service, some urge to fit that service into the well-being of the community--these are the most vital things education must try to produce.

Virginia Gildersleeve
Many a Good Crusade

You must learn day by day, year by year, to broaden your horizon. The more things you love, the more you are interested in, the more you enjoy, the more you are indignant about--the more you have left when anything happens.

Ethel Barrymore

Life

Having grown up in a racist culture where 2 and 2 are not 5, I have found life to be incredibly theatrical and theatre to be profoundly lifeless..

Beah Richards, A Black Woman Speaks

I have a simple philosophy. Fill what's empty. Empty what's full. And scratch where it itches.

Alice Roosevelt Longworth

Rosiness is not a worse windowpane than gloomy gray when viewing the world.

Grace Paley
Enormous Changes at the Last Minute

Loss of Self

A woman obsessed with her body is also obsessed with the limitations of her emotional life.
Kim Chernin, <u>The Obsession</u>

Black women do not yet love ourselves as women. We've been taught to love everyone else; we've been taught, in fact, that it's shameful to love ourselves.
Alexis DeVeaux
quoted in <u>Black Women Writers at Work</u>

A woman who has no way of expressing herself and of realizing herself as a human being has nothing else to turn to but the owning of material things.
Enriqueta Longauex y Vasquez
quoted in <u>Sisterhood is Powerful</u>

Life is a process of becoming, a combination of states we have to go through. Where people fail is that they wish to elect a state and remain in it. This is a kind of death.
Anais Nin
<u>The Anais Nin Reader</u>

I'm suddenly realizing that I've wasted a lot of time just being afraid and just being polite and just holding back and just letting people do just what they want with us.

Mary Tsukamoto on her involvement with
the Japanese-American movement for redress
quoted in <u>Dignity</u>

Troubles, like babies, grow larger by nursing.

Lady Caroline Holland

When we hear jokes against women, and we are asked why we don't laugh at them, the answer is easy, simple, and short. Of course we're not laughing, you asshole. Nobody laughs at the sight of their own blood.

Naomi Weisstein, <u>All She Needs</u>

Love and Sex

I tend to agree that celibacy for a time is worth considering, for sex is dirty if all it means if winning a man, conquering a woman, beating someone out of something, abusing each other's dignity in order to prove that I am a man, I am a woman.

Toni Cade Bambara
"On the Issue of Roles" in <u>The Black Woman</u>

The human need for love and sex is made to bear the burden of all our bodily starvation for contact and sensation, all our creative starvation, all our need for social contact, and even our need to find meaning in our lives.

Deirdre English and Barbara Ehrenreich
quoted in The Women Say/The Men Say

A little coitus wouldn't hoitus.

Graffiti from women's toilets
quoted in Chic 1977

All your gifts should be rainbows if I owned half the shine, and but a bit of sea to furnish raindrops for me.

Emily Dickinson, Letters

Bisexuality is not so much a copout as a fearful compromise.

Jill Johnston, Lesbian Nation

How do you know Love is gone? If you said that you would be there at seven and you get there by nine, and he or she has not called the police yet,--it's gone.

Marlene Dietrich
Marlene Dietrich's ABC

I truly feel that there are as many ways of loving as there are people in the world and as there are days in the lives of those people.

Dr. Mary Calderone, quoted in Ms. 1979

Love between women is seen as a paradigm of love between equals, and that is perhaps its greatest attraction.

Elizabeth Janeway
Between Myth and Morning

Love has the quality of informing almost everything--even one's work.

Sylvia Ashton-Warner, Myself

Sex is like bridge. If you have a good hand, you don't need a partner.

Graffiti from women's toilet
quoted in Chic 1977

The truth is that there is only one terminal dignity--love. And the story of a love is not important--what is important is that one is capable of love. It is perhaps the only glimpse we are permitted of eternity.

Helen Hayes

Two persons love in one another the future good which they aid one another to unfold.

Margaret Fuller
"The Great Lawsuit"

Marriage

A man who is compelled to go on materially and morally supporting a woman he no longer loves feels he is victimized; but if he abandons without resources the woman who has pledged her whole life to him, she will be quite as unjustly victimized.

> Simone de Beauvoir
> The Second Sex

And I knew that in spite of all the roses and kisses and restaurant dinners a man showered on a woman before he married her, what he secretly wanted when the wedding service ended was for her to flatten out underneath his feet like Mrs. Willard's kitchen mat.

> Sylvia Plath, The Bell Jar

Any one must see at a glance that if men and women marry those whom they do not love, they must love those whom they do not marry.

> Harriet Martineau
> Society in America

Next to hot chicken soup, a tattoo of an anchor on your chest, and penicillin, I consider a honeymoon one of the most overrated events in the world.

> Erma Bombeck
> if life is a bowl of cherries, what am I doing in the pits?

The trouble with some women is that they get all excited about nothing--and then marry him.

Cher

I am in truth very thankful for not having married at all.

Harriet Martineau, <u>Autobiography</u>

Men

A man that is ashamed of passions that are natural and reasonable, is generally proud of those that are shameful and silly.

Lady Mary Wortley Montagu
quoted in <u>by a woman writt</u>

There is an incredible amount of magic and feistiness in black men that nobody has been able to wipe out. But everybody has tried.

Toni Morrison
quoted in <u>The Third Woman</u>

Doubt the man who swears to his devotion.

Louise Colet

It is men, not women, who have promoted the cult of brutal masculinity; and because men admire muscle and physical force, they assume that we do too.

Elizabeth Gould Davis, <u>The First Sex</u>

Men who flatter women do not know them;
men who abuse them know them still less.

Madame de Salm

Motherhood

If women once learn to be something themselves
[and learn] that the only way to teach is to be
fine and shining examples, we will have in one
generation the most remarkable and glorious
children.

Brenda Ueland, If You Want to Write

Just as you inherit your mother's brown eyes,
you inherit part of yourself.

Alice Walker quoted in Lear's 1989

The only thing that seems eternal and natural
in motherhood is ambivalence.

Jane Lazarre, The Mother Knot

My mother told me stories all the time, .. And
in all of those stories she told me who I was,
who I was supposed to be, whom I came from,
and who would follow me. In this way, she
taught me the meaning of the words she said,
that all life is a circle and everything has a
place within it. That's what she said and what
she showed me in the things she did and the way
she lives.

Paula Gunn Allen, The Sacred Hoop

The motives behind the universal condemnation of extra-legal motherhood are various and complex; but I believe it is safe to say that the strongest is masculine jealousy.

Suzanne La Follette
Concerning Women

A mother starts out as the most important person in her child's world and if she's successful in her work, she will eventually become the stupidest.

Mary Kay Blakely writing in Lear's 1989

Peace & Understanding

I've been with the best and the worst in my life, and the secret is they're all people.

Helen Drazenovich Berklich
quoted in Dignity

If women ruled the world and we all got massages, there would be no war.

Carrie Snow, quoted in Ms. 1989

Racism, classism, and sexism will disappear when we accept differences and if we continue to resist loudly and clearly all racist, classist and sexist efforts on the part of other persons to enslave us.

Martha Cotera
quoted in The Chicana Feminist

Remember that you are all people and that all people are you.

Joy Harjo quoted in <u>That's What She Said</u>

Small use it will be to save democracy for the race if we cannot save the race for democracy.

Jeannette Rankin

The motto should not be: Forgive one another; rather, understand one another.

Emma Goldman

We have to face the fact that either all of us are going to die together or we are going to learn to live together and if we are to live together we have to talk.

Eleanor Roosevelt

You cannot shake hands with a clenched fist.

Indira Gandhi

Perseverance

An ox at the roadside, when it is dying of hunger and thirst, does not lie down; it walks up and down--up and down, seeking it knows not what;--but it does not lie down.

Olive Schreiner, <u>From Man to Man</u>

Hard times ain't quit and we ain't quit.
Meridel Le Sueur, <u>Salute to Spring</u>

In the turbulence of this anxious and active world many people are leading uneventful, lonely lives. To them dreariness, not disaster, is the enemy. They seldom realize that on their steadfastness, on their ability to withstand the fatigue of dull repetitive work and on their courage in meeting constant small adversities depend in great measure the happiness and prosperity of the community as a whole.
Elizabeth II

Walls have been built against us, but we are always fighting to tear them down, and in the fighting, we grow, we find new strength, new scope.
Eslanda Goode Robeson
quoted in <u>A Day at a Time</u>

We must do the things we think we cannot do.
Eleanor Roosevelt

When you put your hand to the plow, you can't put it down until you get to the end of the row.
Alice Paul

Though I have no productive worth, I have a certain value as an indestructible quantity.
Alice James, <u>Diary</u>

Personal Growth

Any woman who has a great deal to offer the world is in trouble. And if she's a black woman, she's in deep trouble.
Hazel Scott quoted in <u>Ms</u>.

Nothing in life is to be feared. It is only to be understood.
Marie Curie

I don't wish not to be a woman, but I'd certainly like to be a woman whose sense of purpose comes from within.
Uno Chiyo
from "A Genius of Imitation"
quoted in <u>To Live and To Write</u>

I must take the responsibility of standing up for my rights and those of other oppressed people as well. I can only take this responsibility when I have come to terms with my past.
Juanita Ramos

I feel that what we must say to one another is based on encouraging each of us to be true to herself: "Now that we are equal, let us dare to be different!"

Maria de Lourdes Pintasilgo
Sisterhood is Global

It is necessary to try to surpass one's self always; this occupation ought to last as long as life.

Queen Christina

No longer will women agree to protect the hearth at the price of extinguishing the fire within ourselves.

Celia Gilbert quoted in Working It Out

I'm not afraid of storms, for I'm learning how to sail my ship.

Jo in Louisa May Alcott's Little Women

Until we can all present ourselves to the world in our completeness, as fully and beautifully as we see ourselves naked in our bedrooms, we are not free.

Merle Woo
This Bridge Called My Back

One can never consent to creep when one feels an impulse to soar.

Helen Keller, The Story of My Life

*The most frustrating thing about unwelcome
and chronic pain is its mandate to revise your
life. Revision marks a measure of acceptance.
And to accept it feels too much like abandoning
independence.*

Carolyn Hardesty
in <u>With Wings</u>

*There is a confinement and a discipline and
a preparation for leadership that you develop
through being alone, which women are
fearful of.*

Jewell Jackson McCabe
<u>I Dream A World</u>

*You will do foolish things, but do them with
enthusiasm.* Colette

Politicians

*Ninety-eight percent of the adults in this
country are decent, hard-working, honest
Americans. It's the other lousy two percent
that get all the publicity. But then we elected
them.* Lily Tomlin

*When men talk about defense, they always
claim to be protecting women and children,
but they never ask women and children what
they think.*

Pat Schroeder quoted in <u>Ms</u>. 1976

Poverty & Wealth

If these great men must have outdoor memorials let them be in the form of handsome blocks of buildings for the poor.

Elizabeth Cady Stanton, <u>Diary</u>

It is seldom that the miserable of the world can help regarding their misery as a wrong inflicted by those who are less miserable.

George Eliot

The difference between rich and poor is that the poor do everything with their own hands and the rich hire hands to do things.

Betty Smith
<u>A Tree Grows in Brooklyn</u>

Welfare's like a traffic accident. It can happen to anybody, but especially it happens to women.

Johnnie Tilman in <u>Ms</u>. 1972

Power

It is not who you attend school with but who controls the school you attend.

Nikki Giovanni
"One Day I Fell Off the Roof"
in <u>The Black Woman</u>

Women have had the power of naming stolen from us. We have not been free to use our own power to name ourselves, the world, or God.

Mary Daly, Beyond God the Father

A Bitch takes shit from no one. You may not like her, but you cannot ignore her.

Joreen, The Bitch Manifesto

Arbitrary power is like most other things which are very hard, very liable to be broken.

Abigail Adams
quoted in The Feminist Papers

There are questions of real power and then there are questions of phony authority. You have to break through the phony authority to begin to fight the real questions of power.

Karen Nussbaum
quoted in Not Servants, Not Machines:
Office Workers Speak Out

Public Opinion

I cannot and will not cut my conscience to fit this year's fashions.

Lillian Hellman
Letter to the Committee
on UnAmerican Activities

Ideas move fast when their time comes.

Carolyn Heilbrun
Toward a Recognition of Androgyny

It's necessary in order to attract attention, to dazzle at all costs, to be disapproved of by serious people, and quoted by the foolish.

Jill Johnston, <u>Lesbian Nation</u>

The feeble tremble before opinion, the foolish defy it, the wise judge it, the skillful direct it.

Manon Roland

Today's shocks are tomorrow's conventions.

Carolyn Heilbrun
<u>Toward a Recognition of Androgyny</u>

We had to do well and bring no shame to the family name; and although I followed mother's code of behavior for a long time, I don't think I was ever really convinced that it was correct or comfortable. It was simply easier to do than to question why.

Joanne Harumi Sechi
quoted in <u>The Third Woman</u>

Race

Black women have never had an opportunity of displaying our talents; therefore the world thinks we know nothing.

Maria Stewart quoted in
<u>Black Women in 19th Century American Life</u>

Indians think it is important to remember, while Americans believe it is important to forget.

Paula Gunn Allen, The Sacred Hoop

Please stop using the word "Negro,"... We are the only human beings in the world with 57 varieties of complexions who are classed together as a single racial unit. Therefore, we are truly colored people, and that is the only name in the English language which accurately describes us.

Mary Church Terrell
A Colored Woman in a Colored World

Racism is a weapon used by the wealthy to increase the profits they bring in by paying Black workers less for their work.

Angela Davis, Autobiography

Sometimes, it's like a hair across your cheek. You can't see it, you can't find it with your fingers, but you keep brushing at it because the feel of it is irritating.

Marian Anderson on prejudice

There is nowhere you can go and only be with people who are like you. Give it up.

Bernice Johnson Reagon
quoted in Home Girls

We have tilled the fields, planted the cotton and corn, tended the cattle, slopped the hogs, nursed and mothered the young, laid the foundation for the wealth of this country, fought in every way to preserve that wealth and protect the freedom of the land. Now we demand the right to live in freedom and peace, rich in the knowledge that we will henceforth and forever be recognized, not as inferior Negroes but as free Americans.

Sonora McKeller
quoted in <u>From the Ashes: Voices of Watts</u>

It's not because one is black that the prejudice exists. The prejudice exists because one can identify the person who was once a slave or in the lower class, and the caste system can survive longer. In Nazi Germany, they found a way to identify the Jews by putting a label on them to indicate who they were ...They needed a mark. But here you have people who are black people.

Toni Morrison
<u>Conversations With American Writers</u>

Relationships

Life and death occur, as they must, but they are all bound up with love and hatred, in the individual bosom, and it is a sin and a shame to try to organize or dictate them.

Louise A. Bogan, quoted in <u>Ms.</u> 1974

What a commentary on our civilization, when
being alone is considered suspect; when one has
to apologize for it, make excuses, hide the fact
that one practices it--like a secret vice!

Anne Morrow Lindbergh, Gift from the Sea

From the moment we walk out the door
until we come back home our sensibilities are
so assaulted by the world at large that we have
to soak up as much love as we can get, simply
to arm ourselves. It's like going to the gas sta-
tion for a refill. We humans need to hear
'I love you' and we need to hear it as often as
we can.

Patty Duke, Call Me Anna

It is the lesbian in every woman who is
compelled by female energy, who gravitates
toward strong women, who seeks a literature
that will express that energy and strength. It is
the lesbian in us who drvies us to feel imagina-
tively, render in language, grasp, the full
connection between woman and woman.

Adrienne Rich
"It is the Lesbian in Us"
in Lies, Secrets, and Silence

Deafness has left me acutely aware of both the
duplicity that language is capable of and the
many expressions the body cannot hide.

Terry Galloway
in With Wings

Relationships. That's all there really is.
There's your relationship with the dust that
just blew in your face, or with the person who
just kicked you end over end. . . You have to
come to terms, to some kind of equilibrium,
with those people around you, those people
who care for you, your environment.

Leslie Marmon Silko
quoted in The Third Woman

Elinor agreed with it all, for she did not think
he deserved the compliment of rational
opposition.   Jane Austen

My friends are my estate.

Emily Dickinson, Letters

Relationships are like pressures that push you
in 36 directions of the compass. But, as in a
crowded streetcar, if you learn how to maintain your balance against all the weights,
you might arrive at yourself.

Diana Chang
The Frontiers of Love

The love expressed between women is particu-
lar and powerful, because we have had to love
in order to live; love has been our survival.

Audre Lorde "My Words will be There"
in Black Women Writers

The only good teachers for you are those friends who love you, who think you are interesting or very important, or wonderfully funny.

Brenda Ueland
If You Want to Write

Those who trust us educate us.

George Eliot

Remembrance

I love my past. I love my present. I'm not ashamed of what I've had, and I'm not sad because I have it no longer.

Colette, The Last of Cheri

Women and elephants never forget.

Dorothy Parker
Ballade of Unfortunate Mammals

Self-Knowledge

I have a right to my anger, and I don't want anybody telling me I shouldn't be, that it's not nice to be, and that something's wrong with me because I get angry.

Maxine Waters, I Dream A World

Experience is what happens to you in the long run; the truth that finally overtakes you.

Katharine Anne Porter

Even a stopped clock is right twice a day.

Marie Ebner-Eschenbach

I want, by understanding myself, to understand others. I want to be all that I am capable of becoming.

Katharine Mansfield, <u>Journal</u>

If you do not tell the truth about yourself you cannot tell it about other people.

Virginia Woolf
<u>The Moment and Other Essays</u>

It was completely fruitless to quarrel with the world, whereas the quarrel with oneself was occasionally fruitful and always, she had to admit, interesting.

May Sarton
<u>Mrs. Stevens Hears the Mermaids Singing</u>

One certainty we all accept is the condition of being uncertain and insecure.

Doris Lessing
<u>A Small Personal Voice</u>

Our society allows people to be absolutely neurotic and totally out of touch with their feelings and everyone else's feelings, and yet be very respectable.

Ntozake Shange
quoted in <u>Black Women Writers at Work</u>

The woman who endangers the patriarchy is the woman whose love for others grows from her love for herself.

Karen Lindsey
quoted in <u>The Women Say/The Men Say</u>

We've been taught to respect our fears, but we must learn to respect ourselves and our needs.

Audre Lorde
"My Words Will Be There"
in <u>Black Women Writers</u>

Social/Political Movements

Come, come, my conservative friend, wipe the dew off your spectacles, and see that the world is moving.

Elizabeth Cady Stanton
<u>The Woman's Bible</u>

The women and the men of Native America are busily rebuilding their traditions, and the one most in need of rebuilding at this time is the way of the mothers and the grandmothers, the sacred way of the women. When Grandmother returns (and she's coming soon) we want to be ready; we intend to be ready . . . And we are busily stealing the thunder back, so it can empower the fires of life we tend, have always tended, as it was ever meant to.

Paula Gunn Allen
The Sacred Hoop

A lesbian is the rage of all women condensed to the point of explosion.

Radicalesbians
"The Woman-Identified Woman"

Reformers must expect to be disowned by those who are only too happy to enjoy what has been won for them.

Doris Lessing
The Golden Notebook

Let my name stand among those who are willing to bear ridicule and reproach for the truth's sake, and so earn some right to rejoice when the victory is won.

Louisa May Alcott to Lucy Stone, Letters

An extraordinary woman of this century said:
"Women are not born, they're made." I would
like us to ask ourselves: "How do they make us
into women?" and, even more important,
"How do _we_ make women?"

Luz Helena Sanchez
Sisterhood is Global

Being a lesbian is by definition an act of
treason against our cultural values.

Juanita Ramos, Companeras

Cautious, careful people, always casting about
to preserve their reputation and social standing,
never can bring about a reform. Those who are
really in earnest must be willing to be anything
or nothing in the world's estimation, and publicly and privately, in season and out, avow
their sympathies with despised and persecuted
ideas and their advocates, and bear the conse-
quences.

Susan B. Anthony

I always feel the movement is a sort of mosaic.
Each of us puts in one little stone, and then you
get a great mosaic at the end.

Alice Paul
quoted in American Heritage

I am glad to see that men are getting their rights, but I want women to get theirs, and while the water is stirring I will step into the pool.

Sojourner Truth
quoted in <u>The Female Experience</u>

I have met brave women who are exploring the outer edge of human possibility, with no history to guide them, and with a courage to make themselves vulnerable that I find moving beyond words.

Francine Klagsbrun
quoted in <u>The First Ms. Reader</u>

It's fine to coalesce on common issues but the plain fact is we don't want what they want. At least half of the people(men) in this country don't want women to live. Approximately 80% could care less about Black people. Ninety percent(who really knows?) are adamantly opposed to homosexuality. So who is going to fight for our lives but us?

Beverly Smith
"The Wedding" in <u>Home Girls</u>

Lifting as they climb, onward and upward they go struggling and striving and hoping that the buds and blossoms of their desires may burst into glorious fruition ere long.

Mary Church Terrell
quoted in <u>The Voice of Black America</u>

Maybe the people are afraid that if the Indian kids get too well-educated they might try to take this land back. We don't want it after all the damage that has been done to it. All we want is the part that's undamaged and that belongs to us.

Irene Mack Pyawasit
quoted in Dignity

I never doubted that equal rights was the right direction. Most reforms, most problems are complicated. But to me there is nothing complicated about ordinary equality.

Alice Paul
quoted in American Heritage

Our movement is composed of all kinds of groups and all kinds of individuals . . . We must certainly be frank with each other when we disagree, but my plea is that we not begin to be afraid of any of us, in a panic, try to wish any of us out of the picture. We will need every one of us. We are all part of one another.

Barbara Deming
We are All Part of One Another

Our very strength as lesbians lies in the fact that we are outside of patriarchy; our existence challenges its life.

Charlotte Bunch
"Not for Lesbians Only" in Quest

Revolution begins with the self, in the self.
Toni Cade Bambara
The Black Woman

Though people with disabilities have become more vocal in recent years, we still constitute a very small minority. Yet the Beautiful People--the slender, fair and perfect ones--form a minority that may be even smaller.
Debra Kent
in With Wings

There will never be a new world order until women are a part of it.
Alice Paul
quoted in Washington Post 1977

We are in for a very, very long haul . . . I am asking for everything you have to give. We will never give up . . . You will lose your youth, your sleep, your patience, your sense of humor and occasionally, the understanding and support of people who love you very much. In return, I have nothing to offer you but your pride in being a woman, and all your dreams you've ever had for your daughters and nieces and granddaughters. . . your future and the certain knowledge that at the end of your days you will be able to look back and say that once in your life you gave everything you had for justice.
Jill Ruckelshaus, 1977 speech

To die for the revolution is a one-shot deal; to live for the revolution means taking on the more difficult commitment of changing our day-to-day life patterns.

Frances M. Beal
quoted in <u>Sisterhood is Powerful</u>

Today wherever women gather together it is not necessarily nurturing. It is coalition building. And if you feel the strain, you may be doing some good work.

Bernice Johnson Reagon
quoted in <u>Home Girls</u>

But the women we really are can only live if we break open the secret. How many daughters, mothers, sisters, godmothers, and grandmothers, aunts, cousins and best friends have lived and died unknown? Each woman's forced silence was a denial of her existence, as if she never loved another woman, never rejoiced in their union, or cried for her, or waited for her to come home.

Juanita Ramos, <u>Companeras</u>

We haven't come a long way, we've come a short way. If we hadn't come a short way, no one would be calling us "baby."

Elizabeth Janeway

We learn best to listen to our own voices if we are listening at the same time to other women --whose stories, for all our differences, turn out, if we listen well, to be our stories also.

Barbara Deming "Remembering Who We Are"
in <u>We are All Part of One Another</u>

We might well long for the day when the knowledge of the debt all society owed to organized womanhood in bringing the human race closer together, not pushing it farther apart, will still the laughter in the throats of the now uninformed.

Lorraine Hansberry
"In Defense of the Equality of Men"
in<u>The Norton Anthology of Literature By Women</u>

We must not make war on each other while, in our vulnerability, we try to create some-thing new.

Miriam Schapiro
quoted in <u>Working It Out</u>

You have to make more noise than anybody else, you have to make yourself more obtru-sive than anybody else, you have to fill all the papers more than anybody else, in fact you have to be there all the time and see that they do not snow you under, if you are really going to get your reform realized.

Emmeline Pankhurst, <u>My Own Story</u>

Strength of Character

Black women as a group have never been fools.
We couldn't afford to be.

Barbara Smith, Home Girls

Inside myself is a place where I live all alone
and that's where you renew your springs that
never dry up.

Pearl Buck

Fear not those who argue but those who dodge.

Marie Ebner-Eschenbach

Parents can only give good advice or put them
on the right paths, but the final forming of a
person's character lies in their own hands.

Anne Frank, Diary

There's some kind of courage and independence
in a woman who's had to work hard all her life.

Donna Redmond
quoted in Hillbilly Women

Stress

It is not true that life is one damn thing after
another--it's one damn thing over and over.

Edna Saint Vincent Millay, Letters

It's not the tragedies that kill us,
it's the messes.
Dorothy Parker

No day is so bad it can't be fixed with a nap.
Carrie Snow
quoted in <u>Ms</u>. 1989

The trouble with the rat race is that even if
you win, you're still a rat.
Lily Tomlin

Success

Apparent failure may hold in its rough shell
the germs of a success that will blossom in
time, and bear fruit throughout eternity.
Frances Ellen Watkins Harper
quoted in <u>The Voice of Black America</u>

She's OK if you like talent.
Ethel Merman on her friend Mary Martin

Today, a woman needs to forget that she's different or new to something. She simply needs
to do what she does best.
Joan Deal
quoted in <u>Real Estate Today</u>

I always wanted to be somebody. If I made
it, it's half because I was game enough to take
a lot of punishment along the way and half

*because there were a lot of people who cared
enough to help me.*

Althea Gibson

*I really do believe I can accomplish a great deal
with a big grin. I know some people find that
disconcerting, but that doesn't matter.*

Beverly Sills quoted in <u>Ms</u>. 1979

*It is not the destiny of Black America to repeat
white American's mistakes. But we will, if we
mistake the trappings of success in a sick
society for the signs of a meaningful life.*

Audre Lorde "My Words will be There"
in <u>Black Women Writers</u>

*Women share with men the need for personal
success, even the taste for power, and no longer
are we willing to satisfy those needs through
the achievements of surrogates, whether hus-
bands, children or merely role models.*

Elizabeth Dole

*Only on the surface of things have I ever trod
the beaten path. So long as I could keep from
hurting anyone else, I have lived, as completely
as it was possible, the life of my choice. I have
been free. . . I have done the work I wished to
do for the sake of that work alone.*

Ellen Glasgow
<u>The Woman Within</u>

Woman's Role in the World

[Only black women can say] when and where I enter, in the quiet, undisputed dignity of my womanhood, without violence and without suing or special patronage, then and there the whole race enters with me.

Anna Julia Cooper
quoted in When and Where I Enter

Women have been the truly active people in all cultures, without whom human society would long ago have perished, though our activity has most often been on behalf of men and children.

Adrienne Rich, "On History, Illiteracy, Passivity,
Violence, and Women's Culture,"
in Lies, Secrets, and Silence

As a woman I have no country . . . As a woman my country is the whole world.

Virginia Woolf, Three Guineas

A strong woman is a woman at work, cleaning out the cesspool of the ages, and while she shovels, she talks about how she doesn't mind crying, it opens the ducts of the eyes, and throwing up develops the stomach muscles, and she goes on shoveling with tears in her nose.

Marge Piercy

Black women have not historically stood in
the pulpit, but that doesn't undermine the
fact that they built the churches and maintain
the pulpits.

Maya Angelou
quoted in <u>Black Women Writers at Work</u>

How wrong it is for woman to expect the man
to build the world she wants, rather than set out
to create it herself.

Anais Nin, <u>Diary</u> Vol. 5

I like to help women help themselves, as that
is, in my opinion, the best way to settle the
woman question. Whatever we can do & do
well we have a right to, & I don't think any one
will deny us.

Louisa May Alcott, <u>Letters</u>

Is there not a terrible hollowness, mockery,
want, craving, in that existence which is given
away to others, for want of something of your
own to bestow it on?

Charlotte Bronte
quoted in <u>The Female Imagination</u>

There is a hidden fear that somehow, if they are
only given a change, women will suddenly do as
they have been done by.

Eva Figes
<u>Patriarchal Attitudes</u>

This is a time in history when women's voices must be heard, or forever be silenced. It's not because we think better than men, but we think differently. It's not women against men, but women and men. It's not that the world would have been better if women had run it, but that the world will be better when we as women, who bring our own perspective, share in running it.

Betty Bumpers
Conference speech, 1985

Tremendous amounts of talent are being lost to our society just because that talent wears a skirt.

Shirley Chisholm
Unbought and Unbossed

Women are the real architects of society.

Harriet Beecher Stowe

Woman's Worth

Women offer new leadership in an uninspired time, a new supply of energy in a void of scarcity, and the power of our collective spirit in a time of apathy.

Yvonne Burke

*For women there are, undoubtedly, great diffi-
culties in the path, but so much the more to
overcome. First, no woman should say,
"I am but a woman!" But a woman!
What more can you ask to be?*
Maria Mitchell, <u>Life, Letters, and Journals</u>

*Remember, Ginger Rogers did everything Fred
Astaire did, but she did it backwards and in
high heels.*
Faith Whittlesey

*We bear the world and we make it . . . There was
never a great man who had not a great mother.*
Lyndall in Olive Schreiner,
<u>The Story of an African Farm</u>

Work

*Every woman is a human being--one cannot
repeat that too often--and a human being must
have occupation if he or she is not to become a
nuisance to the world.*
Dorothy L. Sayers

*I just don't ever want to give up working.
Honey, I can't.*
Alma Peaster
quoted in <u>Utne Reader</u>

In spite of her supposed segregation to maternal duties, the human female, the world over, works at extra-maternal duties for hours enough to provide her with an independent living, and then is denied independence on the ground that motherhood prevents her working!

Charlotte Perkins Gilman
<u>Women and Economics</u>

People who make some other person their job are dangerous.

Dorothy L. Sayers, <u>Gaudy Night</u>

The women who do the most work get the least money, and the women who have the most money do the least work.

Charlotte Perkins Gilman
<u>Women and Economics</u>

There is perhaps one human being in a thousand who is passionately interested in job for the job's sake. The difference is that if that one person in a thousand is a man, we say, simply, that he is passionately keen on his job; if she is a woman, we say she is a freak.

Dorothy L. Sayers, <u>Gaudy Night</u>

Sources

Alcott, Louisa May. Little Women. Modern Library, 1981.

Allen, Paula Gunn,ed. That's What She Said: Contemporary Poetry and Fiction by Native American Women. Indiana University, 1984.

Allen, Paula Gunn. The Sacred Hoop: Recovering the Feminine in American Indian Tradition. Beacon, 1986.

Anzaldua, Gloria. Borderlands/La Frontera: The New Mestiza. Spinsters/Aunt Lute, 1987.

Ashton-Warner, Sylvia. Teacher. Simon & Schuster, 1986.

Baldwin, Faith. Face Toward the Spring. Rinehart, 1956.

Bambera, Toni Cade. The Black Woman. New American Library, 1974.

Beard, Mary Ritter. Woman as a Force in History. Octagon,1946.

Belenky, Mary et al. Women's Ways of Knowing: The Development of Self, Voice and Mind. Basic, 1986.

Bombeck, Erma. if life is a bowl of cherries, what am I doing in the pits? McGraw-Hill, 1978.

Braden, Waldo, ed. Representative American Speeches, 1974-1975 & 1984-1985. H.W. Wilson, 1975/1985.

Brownmiller, Susan. Against Our Will: Men, Women & Rape. Vintage, 1975.

Buck, Pearl S. My Several Worlds. John Day Company, 1954.

Bunch, Charlotte & Nancy Myron, eds. Class & Feminism. Diana Press, 1974.

Buss, Fran Leeper, comp. Dignity: Lower Income Women Tell of Their Lives and Struggles. University of Michigan, 1985.

Carson, Rachel. Silent Spring. Fawcett, 1978.

Chang, Diana. The Frontiers of Love. Random House,1956.

Chernin, Kim. The Obsession: Reflections on the Tyranny of Slenderness. Perennial Library, Harper & Row,1981.

Chisholm, Shirley. Unbought and Unbossed. Houghton, Mifflin Company, 1970.

Cochran, Jacqueline. The Stars at Noon. Little, Brown, 1954.

Colette. My Mother's House. 1922.

Colette. Cheri & The Last of Cheri. Ballantine, 1982.

Cotera, Martha. The Chicana Feminist. Information Systems Development, 1977.

Culley, Margo, ed. A Day at a Time: The Diary Literature of American Women from 1974 to the Present. Feminist Press reprint, 1985.

Daly, Mary. Beyond God the Father: Toward a Philosophy of Women's Liberation. Beacon, 1973.

Davis, Angela. Autobiography. 1974.

Davis, Elizabeth Gould. The First Sex. Putnam's, 1971.

Davis, Rebecca Harding. Life in the Iron Mills. Feminist Press, 1972.

De Beauvoir, Simone. The Second Sex. Vintage,1974.

Deming, Barbara. We are All Part of One Another: A Barbara Deming Reader. Jane Meyerding, ed. New Society Publishers, 1984.

Dietrich, Marlene. Marlene Dietrich's ABC. Ungar, 1984.

Duke, Patty & Kenneth Turan. Call Me Anna: The Autobiography of Patty Duke. Bantam, 1987.

Dunbar, Alice Moore, ed. Masterpieces of Negro Eloquence. Johnson reprint of 1914 ed., 1970.

Eddy, Mary Baker. Science and Health. First Church, 1875.

Evans, Mari, ed. Black Women Writers: A Critical Evaluation. Anchor Press, 1984.

Figes, Eva. Patriarchal Attitudes. Stein & Day, 1970.

Fisher, Dexter. The Third Woman: Minority Women

Writers of the United States. Houghton Mifflin, 1980.
Fitzgerald, Zelda. Save Me the Waltz. Southern Illinois
University, 1967.
Foner, Philip S., ed. The Voice of Black America.
Simon & Schuster, 1972.
Frank, Anne. The Diary of Anne Frank. Doubleday,
1952.
Giddings, Paula. When and Where I Enter: The Impact
of Black Women on Race & Sex in America. William
Morrow Company, 1984.
Gilbert, Sandra M. and Susan Gubar, eds. Norton
Anthology of Literature by Women: The Tradition in
English. W. W. Norton, 1985.
Gilman, Charlotte Perkins. Carl Degler, ed. Women and
Economics. Harper & Row, 1970.
Glasgow, Ellen. The Woman Within. Harcourt, Brace &
World, 1954.
Goulianos, Joan, ed. by a woman writt:Literature from
Six Centuries by and about Women. Penguin, 1974.
Greer, Germaine. The Female Eunuch. Bantam, 1971.
Heilbrun, Carolyn. Toward a Recognition of Androgyny.
Norton, 1982.
Hurston, Zora Neale. Dust Tracks on a Road. University
of Illinois, 1984.
James, Alice. Edel, Leon,ed. The Diary of Alice James.
Penguin,1982.
Janeway, Elizabeth. Between Myth and Morning.
Morrow, 1974.
Janeway, Elizabeth. Women: Their Changing Roles.
Ayers Company, 1973.
Jason, Philip K. ed. The Anais Nin Reader. Avon, 1974.
Johnston, Jill. Lesbian Nation: The Feminist Solution.
Simon & Schuster, 1974.
Kahn, Kathy, ed. Hillbilly Women. Doubleday, 1973.
Keller, Helen. The Story of My Life. Doubleday, 1954.
Kollwitz, Kathe. Diaries and Letters. Regnery, 1955.
La Follette, Suzanne. Concerning Women. Ayers
Company, 1972.

Lanker, Brian, ed. I Dream a World: Portraits of Black
    Women Who Changed America. Stewart, Tabori, &
    Chang, 1989.
Lazarre, Jane. The Mother Knot. McGraw-Hill, 1976.
Le Sueur, Meridel. Salute to Spring. International
    Publishers,1940.
Lear's magazine, 1989.
Lerner, Gerda. The Female Experience: An American
    Documentary. Bobbs-Merrill,1977.
Lessing, Doris. Paul Schlueter, ed. A Small Personal
    Voice: Essays, Reviews, and Letters. Vintage, 1975.
Lessing, Doris. The Golden Notebook. Simon &
    Schuster, 1962.
Lessing, Doris. The Summer Before the Dark.
    Random, 1973.
Lim, Shirley Geok-lin, Mayuma Tsutakawa, & Margarita
    Donnelly, eds. The Forbidden Stitch: An Asian
    American Women's Anthology. Calyx, 1989.
Lindbergh, Anne Morrow. Gift from the Sea. Pantheon,
    1955.
Mansfield, Katharine. The Journal of Katharine
    Mansfield. Richard West, 1979.
Martin, Del. Battered Wives. Glide, 1976.
Martineau, Harriet. Autobiography. Gregg International,
    reprint of 1877 edition.
Martineau, Harriet. Society in America. Peter Smith
    Publishers, 1968 reprint.
Mead, Margaret. Sex and Temperament. Peter Smith
    Publishers, 1963 reprint.
Millett, Kate. Sexual Politics. Doubleday,1969.
Mitchell, Maria. Life, Letters, and Journals. Ayers
    Company, reprint of 1896 edition.
Moffat, Mary Jane and Charlotte Painter, eds.
    Revelations: Diaries of Women. Random
    House,1974.
Moraga, Cherrie & Gloria Anzaldua, eds. This Bridge

Called My Back: Writings by Radical Women of Color.
Persephone Press, 1981.

Morgan, Robin, ed. Sisterhood is Global: The
International Women's Movement Anthology.
Anchor/Doubleday, 1984.

Morgan, Robin, ed. Sisterhood is Powerful. Vintage,
1970.

Ms. Magazine. The Decade of Women: A Ms. History of
the Seventies in Words and Pictures. Putnam's,
1980.

Ms. magazine v. 1-8, 17(1972-1979, 1989).

Myerson, Joel & Daniel Shealy, eds. The Selected
Letters of Louisa May Alcott. Little, Brown, and Co.,
1987.

Nin, Anais. The Diary of Anais Nin, v. 1, 3, 5.
Harcourt,Brace,Jovanovich, 1975, 1980, 1985.

Paley, Grace. Enormous Changes at the Last Minute.
Farrar, Strauss, & Giroux,1960.

Pankhurst, Emmeline. My Own Story. Greenwood
reprint, 1985.

Plath, Sylvia. The Bell Jar. Bantam, 1971.

Potter, Beatrix. The Journal of Beatrix Potter,1881-
1897. Transcr. Leslie Linder. Warne & Co., 1966.

Quest, v.2,1975.

Radicalesbians, Notes from the Third Year. 1970.

Ramos, Juanita, ed. Companeras: Latina Lesbians
(An Anthology). Latina Lesbian History Project,1987.

Rich, Adrienne. On Lies, Secrets, and Silence. W.W.
Norton, 1979.

Richards, Beah. A Black Woman Speaks. 1974.

Roosevelt, Eleanor. You Learn by Living. Harper &
Row, 1960.

Rossi, Alice. The Feminist Papers. Bantam, 1973.

Ruas, Charles, ed. Conversations with American
Writers. Knopf, 1985.

Ruddick, Sara & Pamela Daniels,eds. Working It Out.
Pantheon, 1977.

Rule, Jane. Lesbian Images. Crossing, 1982.

Saxton, Marsha & Florence Howe, eds. <u>With Wings: An Anthology of Literature by and about Women with Disabilities</u>. Feminist Press, 1987.

Sayers, Dorothy L. <u>Clouds of Witness</u>. Avon, 1969.

Sayers, Dorothy L. <u>Gaudy Night</u>. Avon, 1936.

Schreiner, Olive. <u>From Man to Man</u>. Academy Chicago, 1977.

Schreiner, Olive. <u>The Story of an African Farm</u>. Penguin, 1983.

Schulberg, Budd,ed. <u>From the Ashes: Voices of Watts</u>. New American Library, 1967.

Scott-Maxwell, Florida. <u>The Measure of My Days</u>. Knopf, 1968.

Shapiro, Evelyn & Barry. <u>The Women Say/The Men Say</u>. Dell Publishing,1979.

Smith, Barbara, ed. <u>Home Girls: A Black Feminist Anthology</u>. Kitchen Table Press, 1983.

Smith, Betty. <u>A Tree Grows in Brooklyn</u>. Harper & Row, 1968.

Spacks, Patricia Meyer. <u>The Female Imagination</u>. Avon, 1976.

Stanton, Elizabeth Cady. <u>History of Woman Suffrage, v. 1-6</u>. Arno Press, 1969.

Stanton, Elizabeth Cady. <u>The Woman's Bible</u>. Coalition on Women & Religion, 1974 reprint edition.

Stein, Gertrude. <u>Everybody's Autobiography</u>. Cooper Square 1971 reprint.

Stone, Merlin. <u>Ancient Mirrors of Womanhood.</u> Beacon, 1984.

Tanaka, Yukiko, ed. <u>To Live & To Write: Selections by Japanese Women Writers</u>. Seal Press, 1987.

Tate, Claudia, ed. <u>Black Women Writers at Work</u>. Continuum, 1983.

Tepperman, Jean. <u>Not Servants, Not Machines: Office Workers Speak Out</u>. Beacon, 1976.

Terrell, Mary Church. <u>A Colored Woman in a White World</u>. Ayers Company reprint 1980.

Todd, Mabel Loomis, ed. <u>Letters of Emily Dickinson</u>.

Grosset & Dunlap, 1962.

Ueland, Brenda. If You Want to Write. Graywolf, 1987.

Utne Reader magazine, 1989.

Walker, Alice. In Search of Our Mother's Gardens:
Womanist Prose. Harcourt, Brace, Jovanovich, 1983.

Walker, Alice. Living by the Word: Selected Writings,
1973-1987. Harcourt, Brace, & Jovanovich, 1988.

Walker, Lou Ann. A Loss for Words: The Story of Deafness in a Family. Harper & Row, 1986.

Weil, Simone. Richard Rees, ed. On Science,
Necessity, and the Love of God. Oxford Univ.,1968.

Weisstein, Naomi. All She Needs. Quadrangle, 1973.

Wells, Ida B. Alfreda M. Duster, ed. Crusade for
Justice:The Autobiography of Ida B. Wells.
Univ. Chicago, 1972.

Woolf, Virginia. Monday or Tuesday.

Woolf, Virginia. The Moment and Other Essays.
Harcourt, Brace, & Jovanovich,1952.

Zeidenstein, Sondra,ed. A Wider Giving: Women
Writing After a Long Silence. Chicory Blue, 1987.

Biographical Index

Adams, Abigail(1744-1818) One of the earliest American advocates for women's rights, as evidenced through her fascinating letters to John Adams.

Alcott, Louisa May(1832-1888) Writer popularly famous for her children's books, including Little Women, known also to have written adult fiction and mysteries.

Allen, Paula Gunn(n.a.) Lagune/Sioux/Lebanese-American, prominent scholar, writer, and activist on Native American issues.

Anderson, Marian(1902-) Contralto who became in 1955 the first Black singer to appear at the Metropolitan Opera.

Angelou, Maya(1928-) Writer, activist, and teacher best known for the first volume of her autobiography, I Know Why the Caged Bird Sings(1969).

Anthony, Susan B.(1820-1906) A founding mother of the 19th century women's rights and suffrage movements.

Anzaldua, Gloria(n.a.) Tejana Chicana poet.

Ashton-Warner, Sylvia(1905-1984) New Zealand teacher and novelist remembered for her writing on teaching.

Austen, Jane(1775-1817) British novelist known for her witty novels on domestic manners.

Baldwin, Faith(1893-1978) Prolific writer of fiction, non-fiction, and poetry.

Bambara, Toni Cade(1939-) Writer, editor, teacher and a pioneer in Black women's literature.

Barrymore, Ethel(1879-1959) Stage, screen and television actor, one of the Barrymore family of players.

Beal, Frances M.(n.a.) African-American activist, alumna of the civil rights movement and SNCC, who worked in the 1970s at the National Council of Negro Women.

Beard, Mary Ritter(1876-1958) Social historian and feminist whose Woman as a Force in History later provided the scholarly foundation for women's history.

Berklich, Helen Drazenovich(1914-) Northern Minnesotan born of Yugoslavian immigrants, seen in Dignity(1985).

Blakely, Mary Kay(1940-) Writer, feminist, and former editor of Ms. magazine.

Bogan, Louise(1897-1970) Major lyric poet of her generation, known in later life for her literary criticism.

Bombeck, Erma(1927-) Popular humorist, writer, and speaker noted for her down-to-earth tales about personal life.

Bronte, Charlotte(1816-1855) British novelist(Jane Eyre, 1847) and member of the Bronte family of writers.

Brownmiller, Susan(1935-) Early leader of New York City women's liberation, journalist and author(Against Her Will,1975).

Buck, Pearl S.(1892-1973) Pulitzer Prize-winning author (The Good Earth, 1931) and Nobel Prize-winner noted for her progressive ideas on women's status and on tranforming Asia.

Bumpers, Betty(n.a.) Activist and speaker, founder of PeaceLinks, a grassroots organization.

Bunch, Charlotte(1944-) Highly-respected feminist theorist, lecturer, writer and consultant, notable for her writings on lesbian and international issues.

Burke, Yvonne(1932-) Politician who became the first Black woman elected to the California State Assembly and later served in Congress.

Calderone, Dr. Mary(1904-) Physician, author and lecturer who has received numerous awards applauding her advocacy of "plain talk" about sex.

Cameron, Barbara(n.a.) Contemporary Lakota.

Canady, Alexa(1950-) First Black female neurosurgeon.

Carson, Rachel(1907-1964) Writer and environmentalist who sparked public interest in ecology with Silent Spring.

Carter, Lillian(1898-1983) Colorful Georgia community leader, prominent when son Jimmy Carter was president.

Catherine II(1729-1796) Empress of Russia notable for her progressive views and enlightened policies.

Chang, Diana(1934-) Chinese-American writer.

Cher(1946-) Flamboyant Oscar-winning actor, entertainer.

Chernin, Kim(n.a.) Contemporary California author and pyschologist who writes on issues of women's psychology.

Chisholm, Shirley(1924-) Brooklyn politician who became the first Black woman elected to Congress and later ran for the Democratic Presidential nomination.

Chiyo, Uno(1897-) Japanese writer of fiction.

Christina, Queen(1629-1689) Queen of Sweden 1632-1654, patron of the arts, who abdicated for a solitary life in Rome.

Clark, Francine Julian(n.a.) New York actor and writer first published in the anthology A Wider Giving(1987).

Cochran, Jacqueline(1910-1980) Distinguished aviator, the first woman to break the sound barrier in 1953.

Colet, Louise(1810-1876) French poet popular in her time.

Colette(1873-1954) French novelist famous for her unconventional wiritings and activities. Highly decorated in France.

Cooper, Anna Julia(1858-1964) Prominent voice for Black women's education, born in slavery.

Cotera, Martha(n.a.) Contemporary Chicana writer and educator who writes on Chicana issues.

Craik, Diana Mulock(1826-1887) Popular and prolific Victorian writer of domestic novels, poetry, essays.

Curie, Marie(1867-1934) Polish-French physicist, the first female Nobel Prize winner, who discovered radium and charted radioactivity.

Daly, Mary(n.a.) Radical lesbian-feminist philosopher noted for the memorable Gyn/Ecology(1978).

Davis, Angela(1944-) Black American political activist, radical, and writer.

Davis, Elizabeth Gould(1910-1974) Kansas-born librarian and author of The First Sex(1971).

Davis, Rebecca Harding(1831-1910) Author remembered for her story, "Life in the Iron Mills."

Deal, Joan(n.a.) Contemporary Texas real estate sales manager.

De Beauvoir, Simone(1908-1986) French radical philosopher and feminist; her work The Second Sex(1949) became a cornerstone of late 20th century feminism.

De Girardin, Delphine(n.a.) Early 19th-century French writer.

De Maintenon, Françoise(n.a.) Highly influential second wife of Louis XIV, remembered for her personal letters.

De Salm, Mme. No information available.

De Valois, Marguerite Early 19th-century French woman whose reminiscences appeared in the 1831 Memories.

De Veaux, Alexis(1948-) African-American writer, creative artist and educator.

Deming, Barbara(1917-1984) Lesbian feminist and pacifist, political activist.

Dickinson, Emily(1830-1886) Poet considered by many to be America's finest.

Dietrich, Marlene(1901-) German, later American cabaret singer and screen star distinctive for her sultry, sensual manner.

Dole, Elizabeth(1936-) Republican Cabinet officer often appearing on "women most admired" lists.

Duke, Patty (1946-) Television actor awarded several Emmys for her work as a youthful and mature star.

Ebner-Eschenbach, Marie(1830-1916) Austrian writer of novellas and aphorisms.

Eddy, Mary Baker(1821-1910) Founder of the Church of Christ, Scientist, and the creator of its doctrine.

Ehrenreich, Barbara(1941-) Journalist, author and socialist-feminist who writes on contemporary social issues.

Eliot, George(1819-1880) Pseudonym of Mary Anne Evans. Nonconforming English novelist(Silas Marner, 1861) and poet.

Elizabeth II(1926-) Reigning British monarch known for her frequent international travels.

El Saadawi, Nawal(1930-) Egyptian feminist physician and writer, founder in 1982 of the Pan-Arab Women's Organization.

English, Deirdre(1948-) Leftist writer and journalist known for her 1970s collaborative work with Barbara Ehrenreich.

Figes, Eva(1932-) British writer and feminist whose Patriarchal Attitudes(1970) helped spur British feminism.

Fisher, Dorothy Canfield(1879-1958) Prolific writer of stories and novels. Brought Montessori education to America.

Fitzgerald, Zelda(1900-1948) Personality of the 1920s and writer whose work became co-mingled with that of her celebrated spouse, F. Scott Fitzgerald.

Frank, Anne(1930-1945) Jewish German adolescent whose diary of experiences in hiding from the Nazis gained worldwide and lasting acclaim.

Fuller, Margaret(1810-1850) Writer, feminist and critic active with the New England Transcendentalists. Her Woman in the 19th Century(1845) is a seminal work of American feminism.

Fumiko, Hayashi(1903-1951) Writer, the first woman to achieve popular and critical acclaim for fiction writing in Japan.

Galloway, Terry(n.a.) Contemporary, German-born American writer/activist who gradually lost her hearing when young.

Gandhi, Indira(1917-1984) Indian politician and member of the prestigious Nehru family, assassinated in 1984.

Gibson, Althea(1927-) African-American professional athlete outstanding during the 1950s in both tennis and golf.

Gilbert, Celia(1932-) Feminist, poet, editor, recipient of the Pushcart Prize for 1984-1985.

Gildersleeve, Virginia(1877-1965) As dean of Barnard College 1911-1947, an advocate for women's education and the only female delegate to the UN founding conference.

Gilman, Charlotte Perkins(1860-1935) Lecturer and author whose work Women and Economics(1898) powerfully argues for women's economic independence.

Giovanni, Nikki(1943-) Black American poet, lecturer and author.

Glasgow, Ellen(1873-1945) Novelist focused on Virginia society and highly regarded in her own time.

Goldman, Emma(186901940) Russian-born Jewish anarchist, feminist, writer, and dynamic speaker pilloried as "Red Emma" in the early 20th century.

Greer, Germaine(1939-) Australian writer, actor, lecturer and radical feminist now residing in Europe.

Hansberry, Lorraine(1930-1965) Playwright and civil rights advocate tragically dead of cancer in early middle age. A Raisin in the Sun(1959) was the first play by a black woman to be performed on Broadway.

Hardesty, Carolyn(n.a.) Contemporary graduate student who writes about the disability of rheumatoid arthritis in With Wings(1987).

Harjo, Joy(1951-) Noted Creek poet, writer, teacher and artist living in the Southwest.

Harper, Frances E. W.(1825-1911) Lecturer, author and reformer born of free black parents and considered a pioneer in African-American women's literature.

Hayes, Helen(1900-) Film, stage, and television actor considered the first lady of the American theatre.

Heilbrun, Carolyn(1926-) Author, educator, and leading voice on women's literature.

Hellman, Lillian(1905-1984) Noted playwright and author.

Holland, Lady Caroline(1723-1774) Member of the British aristocracy remembered for her fascinating letters.

Huerta, Dolores No information available.

Hurston, Zora Neale(1901-1960) Accomplished African-American writer and anthropologist who shed light on rural black folklife and speech in novels and stories like Their Eyes Were Watching God(1937).

James, Alice(1847-1892) Invalid member of the James family of writers, known for the journal she kept during the last few months of her life.

Janeway, Elizabeth(1913-) New York City author, journalist, critic, lecturer well-known for her thought-provoking books on women's status.

Johnston, Jill(1929-) British-born American journalist and critic, remembered for Lesbian Nation(1974).

Jordan, Barbara(1936-) Black American former congresswoman, commentator, professor at a Texas university.

Joreen(pseud.) Early women's liberation writer.

Keller, Helen(1880-1968) Advocate for the disabled and author whose path toward overcoming multiple disabilities is memorialized in The Miracle Worker(1964).

Kennedy, Florynce(1916-) Black American attorney and activist renowned for her rapier-like wit.

Kent, Debra(n.a.) Contemporary, free-lance writer who discusses the barriers blind women face in With Wings(1987).

Klagsbrun, Francine(n.a.) Jewish American journalist, editor and writer.

Kollwitz, Kathe(1867-1945) German graphic artist and sculptor notable for her woodcuts and political posters.

La Follette, Suzanne(1893-1983) Journalist, writer, suffragist, libertarian remembered for Concerning Women(1926).

Lazarre, Jane(n.a.) Contemporary author.

Le Sueur, Meridel(1900-) Black-listed author rediscovered in the 1970s for her feminist writings on the Midwest.

Lessing, Doris(1919-) Rhodesian writer whose work often centers on women's independence.

Lewis, Abigail(pseud. of Otis Kidwell Burger,1923-) New York City writer and sculptor.

Lindbergh, Anne Morrow(1906-) Popular author of philosophical novels and journals.

Lindsey, Karen(1944-) Radical feminist writer, editor, poet and journalist.

Longeaux y Vasquez, Enriqueta(n.a.) Contemporary Chicana human services worker and journalist.

Longworth, Alice Roosevelt(1884-1980) Social figure and wit, whose father was president and husband a congressman.

Lorde, Audre(1934-) Black American poet and teacher who writes often on lesbianism and feminist political themes.

MacCabe, Jewell Jackson(1945-) President of the National Coalition of 100 Black Women.

MacLane, Mary(1881-1929) American who wrote about her life in the West.

Mansfield, Katherine(1888-1923) New Zealand writer of short stories whose base was often London.

Martin, Del Lesbian-feminist active in early women's liberation, former editor of The Ladder.

Martineau, Harriet(1802-1876) British writer known for her observations in Society in America(1837).

McKeller, Sonora(1914-) African-American, Chicana, Apache and German actor and activist.

Mead, Margaret(1901-1978) Celebrated anthropologist and prolific writer credited with making anthropology accessible to the public.

Meir, Golda(1898-1978) American, later Israeli politician, prime minister(1969-1974) and international figure.

Merman, Ethel(1908-1984) Singer and Broadway actor remembered for her powerful voice.

Millay, Edna St. Vincent(1892-1950) Pulitzer Prize-winning poet popular in the early 20th century.

Millett, Kate(1934-) Feminist, writer, sculptor and educator, author of the seminal work, Sexual Politics(1970).

Mitchell, Maria(1818-1889) Astronomer and highly-regarded teacher at Vassar who encouraged women to enter science. Known for her discovery of a new comet.

Montagu, Lady Mary Wortley(1689-1762) Literary figure who wrote on women's status and education.

Morrison, Toni(1931-) Popular African-American novelist and writer.

Nin, Anaïs(1903-85) Writer best known for her diaries.

Norton, Eleanor Holmes(1938-) Black American attorney, teacher, and civil rights leader, the first woman to chair the Equal Employment Opportunity Commission.

Nussbaum, Karen(n.a.) Contemporary, founder and executive director of 9 to 5, the Assoc. of Working Women.

Oliphant, Margaret(1828-1897) Scottish writer of novels, criticism, travel commentary and an autobiography.

Orbach, Susie(1946-) British-born Jewish socialist-feminist active as a lecturer and author in England and the US.

Paley, Grace(1922-) Writer and teacher, daughter of Russian Jewish immigrants, known for her short stories.

Pankhurst, Emmeline(1858-1928) Controversial head of an English family of suffragists who led the drive for the British woman's right to vote.

Parker, Dorothy(1893-1967) Writer of verse, plays, prose famous for her wit and keen observations on women's status.
Paul, Alice(1885-1977) Charismatic Quaker and feminist who galvanized the drive for American woman suffrage and later authored the Equal Rights Amendment.
Peaster, Alma(n.a.) Contemporary.
Piercy, Marge(1936-) Prolific popular writer and feminist.
Pintasilgo, Maria de Lourdes(1930-) Portuguese politician and writer and activist nationally and internationally on behalf of women. First female Prime Minister in her land(1979).
Plath, Sylvia(1932-1963) Poet and novelist whose The Bell Jar became a classic of women's liberation.
Porter, Katharine Anne(1890-1980) Writer and teacher best remembered for her novel Ship of Fools(1962).
Potter, Beatrix(1866-1943) Popular British children's writer.
Pyawasit, Irene Mack(n.a.) Elderly Menominee interviewed in Dignity(1985).
Radicalesbians Early women's liberation group in New York.
Ramos, Juanita(n.a.) African-American, Puerto Rican, lesbian-feminist socialist who is a teacher in New York City.
Rankin, Jeannette(1880-1973) Pacifist, suffragist, and Congresswoman remembered as the sole Congressperson to oppose US entry into both world wars.
Reagon, Bernice Johnson(n.a.) Contemporary, Black American scholar and member/founder of the musical group Sweet Honey in the Rock.
Redmond, Donna(n.a.) Contemporary quoted in Hillbilly Women(1973).
Reid, Coletta(n.a.) Contemporary lesbian feminist writer, former staffer at Quest, off our backs, and Diana Press.
Repplier, Agnes(1855-1950) Prolific essayist and biographer noted in her time for her writings on English literary history.
Rich, Adrienne(1929-) Poet, teacher, winner of the National Book Award and powerful voice of radical lesbian feminism.
Richards, Beah(n.a.) Film, stage, and television actor and poet elected to the Black Filmmakers Hall of Fame.
Robeson, Eslanda Goode(1896-1965) African-American reformer, lecturer, and writer whose progressive views on colonialism and race and visibility as well as her marriage to singer Paul Robeson gave her notoriety.
Roland, Manon(1754-1793) French democrat and activist during the Revolution, known for her salon.

Roosevelt, Eleanor(1884-1962) Widely-admired defender of the disadvantaged. In later life, an accomplished advocate of human rights and the first chair of the federal Commission on the Status of Women established in 1961.

Ruckelshaus, Jill(n.a.) Contemporary women's liberation advocate married to Cabinet officer William B. Ruckelshaus.

Rule, Jane(1931-) American writer and critic living in British Columbia.

Sanchez, Luz Helena(n.a.) Contemporary Colombian psychotherapist, founded the first feminist group in her land.

Sanger, Margaret(1879-1966) Founder of the birth control movement in the US and an important backer of the development of the Pill in the 1960s.

Sarton, May(1912-) Prolific author of novels, journals, and poetry who writes about the independent life and the relationships between and among women.

Sayers, Dorothy L.(1893-1957) English writer of detective fiction and advocate of women's independence.

Schapiro, Miriam(1923-) Noted artist and educator concerned with writing women into art history.

Schreiner, Olive(1855-1920) South African novelist.

Schroeder, Pat(1940-) Colorado Congresswoman, co-chair of the Congressional Caucus on Women's Issues, and Presidential primary candidate in 1988.

Scott, Hazel(1920-) Black American pianist and international entertainer whose heyday spanned the 1940s & 1950s.

Scott-Maxwell, Florida(1884-) American writer, suffragist, psychologist who lives mostly in Britain.

Sechi, Joanne Harumi(n.a.) Contemporary Japanese-American writer.

Shange, Ntozake(1948-) African-American poet, playwright, teacher and lecturer best known for her 1976 play, "For Colored Girls . . ."

Silko, Leslie Marmon(1948-) Laguna, Mexican and Caucasian writer highly regarded for her writings on the Native American experience.

Sills, Beverly(1929-) Operatic soprano, former director of the New York City Opera and advocate for the disabled.

Smeal, Eleanor(1939-) Charismatic former president of NOW and founder of Fund for the Feminist Majority.

Smith, Barbara(1946-) Black lesbian writer, member/founder of Combahee River Collective and Kitchen Table Press.
Smith, Betty(1896-1972) Novelist remembered for A Tree Grows in Brooklyn(1943).
Smith, Beverly(1946-) Black lesbian writer, twin to Barbara Smith above.
Smith, Patti(1947-) Rock singer and poet.
Snow, Carrie(n.a.) Contemporary feminist comedian.
Stanton, Elizabeth Cady(1815-1902) One of the founding mothers of the 19th century women's rights movement and an organizer of the first convention on women's rights in 1848.
Stark, Freya(1893-) British traveller and writer noted for her observations of the Arab world(Dust in the Lion's Paw,1961).
Stein, Gertrude(1874-1946) Expatriate Jewish-American writer and lesbian who experimented with non-linear narrative.
Steinem, Gloria(1934-) Journalist, activist, a leading light of American liberal feminism, and a founder of Ms. magazine.
Stewart, Maria(1803-1879) Black American abolitionist and feminist well-known as a lecturer in her time.
Stone, Merlin(1931-) Writer and former sculptor who writes on women and spirituality.
Stowe, Harriet Beecher(1811-1896) Author and abolitionist remembered for the success of Uncle Tom's Cabin(1852).
Terrell, Mary Church(1863-1954) Civil rights reformer, suffragist, and first president(later honorary president for life) of the National Association of Colored Women.
Thomas, Marlo(1938-) Feminist, actor-producer, and public figure known to feminists for her Free To Be . . . publications.
Tilman, Johnnie(n.a.) Contemporary, chair of the National Welfare Rights Organization in the early 1970s.
Tomlin, Lily(1939-) Comedian and feminist given numerous awards for her stage, television and recording work.
Truth, Sojourner(1797-1883) Preacher, abolitionist and mystic born Isabella Van Wagener to slaves in New York City.
Tsukamoto, Mary(1915-) Japanese-American living in California, involved with the movement to redress the grievances of Japanese-Americans who were sent to detention camps during World War II.
Ueland, Brenda(c.1892-c.1985) Minneapolis writing teacher and author.

Walker, Alice(1944-) African-American writer of novels, short stories and essays who received the Pulitzer Prize for The Color Purple(1983).

Walker, Lou Ann(1952-) Editor, author, sign language interpreter and consultant who chronicled her young life as a hearing child of deaf parents in A Loss for Words(1986).

Waters, Maxine(1938-) Black American California politician influential in state Democratic politics.

Weil, Simone(1903-1943) French philosopher and writer whose works, all published posthumously, detail her profound identification with the poor.

Weisstein, Naomi(n.a.) Psychology Ph.D., professor and activist who wrote the classic women's liberation essay "Psychology Constructs the Female"(1969).

Wells, Ida B.(1862-1931) Journalist and lecturer born to slave parents who later galvanized America against lynching in the South.

West, Mae(1892-1980) Comedian notorious for her scripts and stage and screen performances which flaunted her sexuality.

Whittlesey, Faith(1939-) Attorney, diplomat, former White House staff member and ambassador to Switzerland.

Whitton, Charlotte(1896-1975) Canadian government official, Mayor of Ottawa for two terms in the 1950s and 60s.

Woo, Merle(n.a.) Contemporary, Asian-American writer, scholar and teacher.

Woolf, Virginia(1882-1941) British author revered for her writings on women's status and read about for her bisexual and otherwise unconventional lifestyle.

Yalow, Rosalyn(1921-) Medical physicist, winner of the 1977 Nobel Prize for medicine and physiology.

Biographical information was not available on every woman quoted in these pages. Information utilized was the best available at the time of publication. All are/were American unless otherwise noted. Race and ethnicity were included when available. Sexual preference was included when publicly acknowledged by the subject or in another source.

For more information, see Notable American Women(James, ed., 1971; Sicherman ed., 1980) or the International Dictionary of Women's Biography(Uglow ed., 1982).

Name Index